Leopards

Patricia Kendell

RAINTREE
STECK-VAUGHN
PUBLISHERS

A Harcourt Company

Austin   New York
www.raintreesteckvaughn.com

Alligators   Chimpanzees   Dolphins Elephants
Gorillas   Grizzly Bears   Leopards   Lions
Pandas   Polar Bears   Sharks   Tigers

Published by Raintree Steck-Vaughn Publishers, an imprint of Steck-Vaughn Company

Library of Congress Cataloging-in-Publication Data is available upon request

ISBN 0-7398-5496-8

Printed in Hong Kong. Bound in the United States.

1 2 3 4 5 6 7 8 9 0 LB 07 06 05 04 03 02

Photograph acknowledgments:
Anup Shah/naturepl.com 11; Bruce Coleman cover & 4 (Alain Compost), 25 (Rod Williams), 28; Ecoscene 24 (Robert Baldwin), 21 (E J Bent), 22 (Lindegger), 17 (Kjell Sandved); FLPA 26 (Michael Gore), 9, 10 (Mark Newman), 5 (Philip Perry), 7 (Fritz Polking), 13 & 32 (Sunset); NHPA 8 (J & A Scott); OSF 14-15 (Daniel Cox), 27 (Colin Monteath), 19 (Richard Packwood), 6 (Mary Plage), 20 (Rafi Ben-Shahar), 12 (Steve Turner); Science Photo Library 18, 23 (Peter Chadwick), 29 (Gregory Dimijian); WTPix 16 (Steve White-Thomson).

Contents

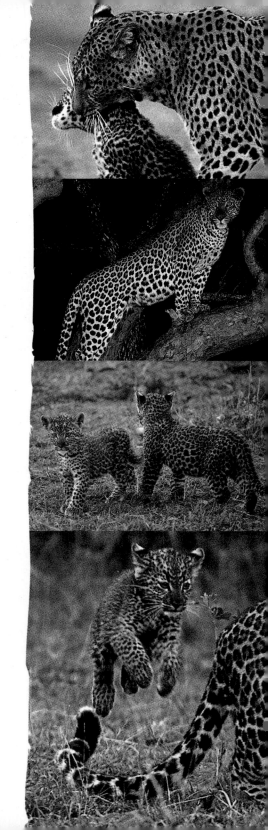

Where Leopards Live

Leopards can be found in parts of Africa and Asia. They are able to live in many different places such as grasslands or in the **rain forest**.

Some leopards survive even in **desert** areas.

Baby Leopards

Two or three **cubs** are born in a **den**.
Newborn cubs are tiny and helpless.

The cubs stay close to their mother. They
drink her milk to grow big and strong.

Looking After the Cubs

Mother leopards keep their cubs clean
by licking them all over.

If there is danger, a mother leopard will gently
carry the cubs to a safer place.

Growing Up

When they are eight weeks old,
the cubs leave the den.

As they grow older, the cubs learn how to hunt
by playing and pouncing on their mother's tail.

Leaving Home

The young leopards leave their mother when they are about two years old.

Once they are grown up, leopards live alone
in a **territory** of their own. They only come
together to **mate**.

On the Move

Like all big cats, leopards can run
and jump easily and **gracefully**.

Their powerful chests and front legs also help them to climb trees easily.

Food

Leopards will kill and eat many different kinds of animal in their territory, like these **impala** and zebra.

Leopards are very good climbers. They often drag their **prey** up a tree. Not many other animals can reach the meal up here.

Out of Sight

The pattern and color of a leopard's fur makes it hard for prey animals to spot it.

18

Leopards have long whiskers to help them
feel their way around when it gets dark.

Hunting

Most leopards hunt at night. Some creep up
and pounce on their prey.

Other leopards climb trees and wait for animals to pass by. Then they jump down on their prey from above.

Night and Day

Leopards are active mainly at night.
They can see very well in the dark.

They usually sleep all day in a tree, especially
if it is hot, or after they have eaten a big meal.

Threats

It is against the law to hunt leopards, but some people kill them and sell their fur.

Today, there are very few Persian leopards
left because too many of them have been
hunted for their beautiful fur.

Dangers

People are cutting down trees and taking the leopards' territory to grow food.

Some farmers poison hungry leopards
to stop them from killing farm animals.

27

Helping Leopards to Survive

Tourists will pay to see animals in the wild.
This is one way that local people can earn
money without killing leopards.

If people look after the forests and mountains, and find ways of sharing them with leopards, then more leopards will survive in the future.

Further Information

Find out more about how we can help leopards in the future.

ORGANIZATIONS TO CONTACT

WWF
1250 24th Street, N.W.
P.O. Box 97180
Washington, D.C. 20037
Tel: (800) CALL-WWF

International Snow Leopard Trust
4649 Sunnyside Avenue North
Suite 325
Seattle, Washington 98103
Tel: (206) 632-2421

Leopards, Etc.
P.O. Box 430
Occidental, CA 95465
Tel: (707) 874-3176

BOOKS

Mead, Katherine. *Why the Leopard Has Spots*. New York: Raintree Steck-Vaughn Publishers, 1997.

Radcliffe, Tessa. *The Snow Leopard*. New York: Puffin Books, 1996.

Schaefer, Lola. *Leopards: Spotted Hunters (Wild World of Animals)*. Minnetonka, MN: Capstone Press Inc., 2001.

Scott, Jonathan. *The Leopard Family Book (Animal Families)*. San Francisco, CA: North South Books, 1999.

St. Pierre, Stephanie. *Leopards (In the Wild)*. Chicago, IL: Heinemann Library, 2001.

Glossary

WEBSITES

Most young children will need adult help when visiting websites. Those listed have child-friendly pages to bookmark.

http://www.leopardsetc.com/meet.html
Children can hear the leopards roar and find out about them in text and photographs.

http://www.kidsplanet.org/factsheets/ snow_leopard.html
This website provides information about, and photographs of, snow leopards.

http://snowleopard.org/islt/classroom
This website has quizzes, games, and slide shows. There is also information about how children can help the endangered snow leopard.

cubs – (KUHBS) the name for baby leopards.

den – (DEN) a wild animal's home.

desert – (DEZ-urt) a very dry place where few trees grow.

graceful – (GRAYSS-ful) to move in a smooth, flowing way.

impala – (im-PAL-uh) a small deer.

mate – (MATE) when male and female leopards come together to make babies.

prey – (PRAY) an animal hunted by another animal for food.

rain forest – (RAYN FOR-ist) forests in hot, wet places.

territory – (TER-uh-tor-ee) the home area of an animal.

Index